NUDE:

Tales of an Enchanted Heart

———

by

Dhakeria Cunningham

NUDE

Nude: Tales of an enchanted heart, by Dhakeria Cunningham. Published 2011 by Evoleno Publishing, LLC., US. © 2011 by Dhakeria Cunningham. The book author retains sole copyright to his or her contributions to this book. No part of this publication may be reproduced, stored in a retrieval system, or transmitted in any form or by any means, electronic, mechanical, recording or otherwise, without the prior written permission of Dhakeria Cunningham.

NUDE

Dedication

To the many warrior women that I've come across in my short existence; the women, who have paved the way for creativity to come forth, especially from unexpected sources; who did not let any extraneous factors disrupt the stasis of their creativity; who never got distracted from the journey; whose focus was unwavering; whose power and strength proved too great for resistance and too solid for the enemy; who realized their beauty, strength and spirituality; who stood firmly and held a strong hand to help the next sister in line; who promoted peace and lived congruently; who made positivity a real life companion; who takes God at his Word and blesses Him daily; who makes a conscious effort to build a relationship with Him and be used by Him; who is not ashamed; who cannot be shamed

To my organizations; Alpha Phi Omega (Zeta Phi), and D.I.V.A., Incorporated, whose brotherhood and sisterhood help build me up in such a profound way, teaching me the value of community and enrichment, showing me limitless possibilities, redefining my potential and negating the odds, helping me to be greater in all aspects, making me stretch my creativity and intellect too far to still be in the box, motivating me to Be a Leader, Be a Friend, and Be of Service and helping me find finer creativity within [my]self, [my] soul, and [my] craft…to the XV(Spartans), the finest set of LBs in existence, PHIIIII QUUUUE! To the Dolls, the most talented group of women that saturates my creative soul! AVID!

To my family; who always see perfection and beauty, who always support my wild and vivid dreams, who have only encouraged me and

NUDE

has never looked down on me, who holds the secret to my successes, who motivates my drive and passion, who are my roots and from whence my talent comes, for the testimonies told during family gatherings that encourage my soul, for maintaining family ties and unbroken bonds, who remains grounded, who has showed me the meaning of togetherness and community, who has always been strong

To my parents; who have provided a solid foundation, made me stronger, gave me room to grow, taught me the measures and value of hard work, taught me to never give up, made me see the bigger picture, made me take off the training wheels, showed me the importance of confidence, instilled the necessity of education and excelling, who has allowed me to think for myself, who prepared me for diversity and adversity

To my sisters Rae and Chipmunk for the bond we share that got us through a bout of hardships; a bond we have all depended on to redeem ourselves and catch back up to being the young women we were drifting away from becoming; for keeping me on track; for noticing my distress calls even if ever so soft; for giving me everything I needed when I was drowning in a sink hole; for always comforting me; for always making me laugh insanely; for pretending with me; for dreaming with me, for always keeping it real; for always believing in me, for looking up to me and making me be a better woman to lead by example, for always showing true hues and for helping me to realize my power

To my other half, indoctrinated member of the Dynamic Duo, the man who has stood by my side and together we have weathered many storms, for taking the time to know me inside and out, for spending countless hours helping me get to my best, for being so supportive and faithful, for being my ROCK, for being understanding, for letting me

NUDE

breathe, for being a good and honest man, for seeing the vision with me, for building a family with me, for letting me be bossy, for seeing past my inconsistencies and imperfections and always looking at me as who I can be, for looking into my soul and reaching from inside there to encourage me, for your diligence and PATIENCE, for your soft resistance, for your brilliance and focus, for being grounded and driven, for being as passionate as me, for making me go there, for walking with me, for your heartbeat (literally), for always holding me down, for being an Amazing Father

To my daughter Zhaniya, who has been my fresh start, my new beginning, for making live, for giving me a new take on life; To my daughter who has shown me through her innocence the beauty and joys of life, who makes everything better with a smile; whose interest in the most minute things prompts me to be grateful for the little things; who inspires me to reach my goals, who makes me reevaluate and reposition myself, to a little girl whose life in and of itself is a blessing to me, for recalibrating my thinking and pushing me forward, for making me realize some of my reasons are excuses, for helping me to know a love so strong/ you trump all materialistic things, all unnecessary ventures/ you make things that are small seem very big and some things I thought were big you made them small/ thank you for choosing me/ I'm eternally grateful and proud to be your mommy my darling baby girl!

To the Most High, an on-time God, for being patient with your child, for the many undeserved blessings, for the favor, for the countless life jackets, for giving me testimonies, for creating me to be a Woman of many talents, for breathing life into the monumental events I've been so fortunate to experience, for never giving up on me when I gave up on myself, for inviting me to those private moments where I can be revived, for teaching me to encourage myself, for being God all by yourself

NUDE

Table of Contents

Foreword 12
Acknowledgements 14
Introduction 15
Nude 17
Interrogation 19
Matters of the heart 21
Out there 21
Realize beauty 22
Beauty Queen 23
What Daydreams May Come 24
Don't bother me none 25
Suspension 26
Starting New 27
I been loving you 28
Evolution's creation 29
Southern Goddess 30
In the nude 32
Contentious Repentance 33
Feeling myself 34
Hold us down (an ode to hip hop) 36
What things could be 38

NUDE

So Sick	39
Guessing	40
Late night	42
Suspended in time	43
Wild flower	44
A disappointment	45
Sister to sister	46
Positive	47
Nights without You	48
Addict	49
Love lead the way	50
Too young to grow	51
Love reality	53
Jazz got the blues	54
Iniquitous cry	55
Soulmate	56
Grace&Mercy personified	57
Love to be made	58
Burnt out/wildfire	59
Flight pattern	61
love twin	61
God's work	61
Tempted	62
Passion	62

NUDE

Unclaimed property	63
Government assistance	63
Done	64
Second Chance	64
Re-religion	65
With a smile	66
The ending?	66
Freely freeing me	67
True beauty virtue	69
Assurance	70
Preggers	70
More Preggers	70
Nauseous	71
Body thoughts	72
Sleepless nights	73
AWAY	74
Take lead	75
Far away form home	76
Conscious living	77
Black Ice	78
GN & GM	78
Answer to My Rebellion	79
Remembering you	81
First day of school	82

NUDE

That's Life	83
Finding perfect	84
Ladylike	85
walkin' holy	85
Mixed breed	86
I. Love. You	87
Winter happenings	87
Country winter	87
Mind made up	88
Reproduction	88
Romanced	89
Completely Incomplete	89
DeVIRGINated	90
Finding u	91
About us	91
Winter Night	92
Overdose	93
Winter Night 2	93
Cold outside	94
Old sins	94
Systemic Waste	96
Road to Stardom	98
Transformed...a poem about motherhood	100

NUDE

NUDE

NUDE

Foreword
by: Evangelist Mildred McMillian

My life's work has been to educate, inspire, and spread the Word of God. My testimonies are infused with crash and burn scenarios and stories of humble beginnings. Ergo, I am ripe with wisdom and experience. It is my responsibility as an elder to pass along this wisdom and teach the younger ones. Our family is rather large, so you can imagine the many children that I've watched grow up and had a hand in molding. Everyone, at one point or another has come through my household, whether to live or spend nights playing with my children. I have been Aunt Mil to many, many family members, some of which I am truly a distant cousin. We were just that close. In a very small town called Eastover, it's hard to walk any street and walk by a house where family doesn't reside. From a very young age my granddaughter has learned the importance of family. She has seen first hand that "it takes a village." Her community has always consisted of family that does things together, from daily gatherings to formal ones like Thanksgiving and Christmas. We all get together and have a good time, telling old stories over and over. Laughing and playing games are a few of the things we like to do. However, eating soul food is the prime activity that brings us together. This is where she developed a love for story telling. Being among the many children in the family, Dhakeria has always shown an interest in the performing arts, often giving us too many dates to remember, all being performances. She was always one with an act or a show. Her religious background gave her the strong foundation for some of her theatrical roots. She was in the church choir and a liturgical

NUDE

dancer. Always eager to take on the challenge, she never gave an attitude or turned me down when I asked her to dance for the congregation in church on the program. I've prophesized over her, knowing the future that awaits her. I just encourage her to always put God first and do all things as if she's doing it unto God. I am truly proud. You are in for a treat as this young lady speaks to your heart.

NUDE

Acknowledgments

I'd like to acknowledge those who have pushed for this book to happen; my newfound brother-in-law Miguel for is diligence and willingness to take me on and publish this work of poetry, my homie-lover-friend William for keeping me on task, my sisters; Torae' for her input, always listening to every poem I write and Torae' AND Bre for lending their talents to the book through illustration, and Niya for keeping me up at night and inspiring me to be greater, go farther, and dig deeper.

NUDE

Introduction

Nude...sounds a bit suspect, maybe derogatory, but it sums up the process of revelation that it has taken to get to this point. This woman has chosen to bare her soul in respect to a few components of the process including love, becoming a mother, moments of self-discovery, maturation and the pangs therein. Emotionally spun, she has gathered the words to describe some of the turbulence this journey has created. Bound by a sense of duty, she has poured her soul into words and let them arrange themselves to tell the stories and testify to the hidden treasures of her enchanted heart.

She began writing as a means of simply organizing her thoughts for verbal fluidity. Then she realized that her thoughts were more creative than simple plain-talk. As she read books and articles, she likened her thoughts to poetic phrasing with Shakespearean beauty and complexity. Her deep thoughts penetrated her mind with ambitious fervor and evacuated her with a certain power. She didn't want to just say the words, they needed more than a voice. They needed a performance. The words were meant to dance from the tongue, dance in the mind, be wrapped in character and professed with profession. The words needed a stage. With all the emotions and passion in her Dhakeria needed to perform. She wanted to act out life's commonalities and give them specific domain, unveil the complexities therein and highlight the uniqueness that creates individuality. She wanted to do this from the same place the words came, from a place of deep-seated passion and dedication, earnest reflection and sincere concentration. She is an artist with a powerful voice a committed heart and a vivid imagination. She needs to create to stay alive. If she cannot create she would be dead...

NUDE

breathing, walking and talking, but void of passion, useless energy and no presence.

In her world, everything is inspiration. Everything has a story. She has a distinct sensitivity to life and creation. At times she feels like an empath, feeling others' pain and discomfort. So she performs each character keeping in mind those specific feelings and detailed emotions, compelled to tell the truth. Her poems are a direct reflection of this need to tell the truth, remaining true to the life, the moments, the thoughts. Hoping to pull someone else up, to inspire and rescue someone who may be going through, she lends her voice and body as a vessel. She uses her gifts she aspires to build a strong foundation for her family, a network of support for anyone in suffering, feeling confused and alone, as empowerment to give someone an extra boost, as a platform for community outreach, and a platform for artistic expression.

At moments in her life when her world seemed to be closing in on her and her airways were so blocked she couldn't scream out, a pad and pen has been her refuge as she writes through the pain and inscribes a path through the thick of the guilt, shame, feelings of self-doubt, hurt, self-loathing, and confusion. She composes an exit sign and transcribes the exit strategy.

The journey to this place is a part of a bigger journey, a deeper path. There's so much more to learn, more to do, more to give, more to be given, farther to travel, higher to climb and farther to reach.

Enjoy your front row seats!

NUDE

Nude

Here I stand naked marked blemished bruised and desperate
Hardly perfect
And I am without shame
The queen of confrontation and dictation becomes my nature
Whether he who holds me in the palm of his hand relinquishes me to he who has not, I am graced to be she who is reputable and beyond gravity
I am delicate, walking the shells of eggs
Unbroken but broken, and love knows me by name
I am without shame, though I cower at the mention of fame
I am known and unknown
Stares gawking sneer jeers persnickety whispers
I hear you
I see you speak not to but of
Of me
Dare you?
I ain't got all day
I got time to pay not play
Time that has stolen from me moments
And given me rapture-like constructions of loveless nights
Oh, how sweet
Loveless…
My heart full of love and light, so this love can land and this love can take flight
I am driven to madness
The insanity settling between my thighs
Can't even get a rise

NUDE

Where's my clothes?
I don't want to be seen so fragile, so insecure
I play myself
In the wind, I throw phrases
Things I can say but once, and live in complete opposition
Stuck in transition
Whining and complaining
A woman, in training
Don't judge me
Love honor and obey me
I hate you
No I love you
But I hate you
Call my bluff before I date you
Come correct before I rate you
Oh my God, I don't know
See I'm stuck in transition
Don't know how to play my position
Where's my clothes so you don't have to see my like THIS
So you can't see my in between stages
I don't want the unfinished to show
You can't see me grow
Can't I just be known after I'm full grown?

NUDE

Interrogation

How you gon'…

Make these pancakes if it's on the floor?
X o x o circle circle dot dot
Ain't no code to this frozen solid chunk of Human Heart
Beating silently in this warm body I feel my life force going limp
And I seep deep in desolation and the isolation remedies
My scream, my shudders, my realizations of real inflations
Of heart matters don't shit matters
Do I matter collateREAL damaged goods
You just gon' put this genie in her bottle
Bottle up the last of this heartbreak-humidity
Humidity mangled by dog-lust you must
Remember that the dog chased the cat where you at
Kitty cat burned and bruised and broken and broken
Cat done got chased up a tree she tryna get free
And free she will be…

How you gon'…

Eat these eggs? Off the floor? A debate of a delicate delegate I have no need for…
Sure of being unsure/ married to the mystery /that lay claim in my present domain
Clearly ruffled by insane accusations/ abbreviations of long extended phrases/
Less capable of singsong melody/ and I perspire profusely through each beat/

The weak of opportunity/
Monday Tuesday Wednesday girl

In her Sunday pearls

NUDE

Looking like a Saturday night girl
In a brave new world/
Looking for where her Thursday and Friday nights went/
All tucked up nice in your sheets/
Shreds of innocence buried deep/ with the bed bugs/
Sweet perspiration that she kept through to the new day/
Finding it familiar/ a million new breaths
    Held in contempt

NUDE

Matters of the heart

Confessedly and with as great an opportunity than ever before

I commissioned the heavens to reveal to me how my love is to be spent and the heavens reply…

To be spent amongst a thousand pennies cast into a wishing well/
Well wishing those who wish well/
Spent amongst a field of lilies laying low beneath the heavens/
Amongst jasmine and clover spent over and over/
My love is to be spent where it cannot be returned back to an empty heart

Out there

Outta control

I'm losing mind

This love is so real

A love I can't find

It hurts me so bad

My knees are so week

This is so deep

I cannot speak...

NUDE

Realize beauty

Hey you
You there in the mirror
How dare you lower your head in shame
Your beauty is uncanny to think less is just lame
Don't you know the image in which you've been created
Your beauty inside and out is worth such that can't be traded
Thus I speak truth and this truth can't be evaded
Your body is fine
Anyone saying different, honey pay them no mind
Only your confidence is left to find and let shine
Wipe those tears away with the grace of a swan
You can swirl into a new day with no magic word or wand
Look above and beyond your doubt
Knowing you're a gift and that's what loving yourself is all about
Step out on faith and know you cannot fail
Become one with the greatness from which you hail
Don't look back forward projection is your only choice
Then once you've made it then you look back and rejoice
You're made of everything you need to succeed
Your dreams aren't fantasies and that's the mindset to feed
Not negativity and thoughts of rejection
Those thoughts plague your life and fill it with deceased infection
Remember it's not who you are but whose you are
Collect your conscious and raise the bar
Higher heights should constantly be in your sights
Walking in your destiny is in your book of rights
Soar in your thoughts and your actions too
When I say you're beautiful and you can make it all I wanna hear from you is...true!

NUDE

Beauty Queen

There she is in her infinite beauty

Her royalty lays her trail and oh how gorgeous the way she's made/
Groomed and polished dipped in luscious scents of ordained glory/
A woman no less/ and grand in presence she blooms buds of
youthful indulgence and brightens lands near and far/
Great is her fervor and brilliance sheens the magnificence of her
skin/ as her light becomes an oasis/ showing how to lead/
She bleeds gold/ touching her face creates ecstasy/ ecstatic in her
body/ boldly benign in it's harm and malign it's affect on lovers/
and fiendishly functions of immortality/ she is the corner place
where love is captured trapped and resides within the longevity of
it's dwelling/ all love resides within her and she abounds with
grace to send it out to the world

Let all the lands know of her beauty/ let all hearts know her love/
and utter the ecstasy of her name built in the glory of her essence
    As she grows and becomes her

NUDE

What Daydreams May Come

The honey dripping from supple breasts
The honeydew scent from fresh fed breath
A Begging
A yearning
The muffled moans of manifestation
You look at me and the lust look penetrates my pupils as love penetrates my soul
I'm taken by the sly smile of sheer satisfaction
Knowing that where we've been/
The journey we have taken/ has given way to the road we have yet to travel
The destiny of us is unknown
And content as we may be, there's much more to learn and far more to grow from
Grown-ups/ age appropriate/ for the touching kissing and what we did/ what we do/ the mint condition of treatment/ the canopy of aggressive love making/ over powering the just so sensual nature of our becoming/
Drumming out the movement/ the rhythm/ the beat/ the heat/
We run into the fog of what we meant
This must be the winter of our discontent
But as we take course over where we have been/ the place we went
We give thanks and pause for a moment to vent
Our past mistakes and heartbreaks
Blatant misuse misconduct and abuse
Relentless invention of misdirected attention and
Mislead convention
You're my distraction availing beyond attraction
Perfecting each moment and propelling my action
    My breath suspends in time/ caught up in the school bell/ and waiting for detention.

NUDE

Don't bother me none...

Don't bother me none that they don't know my name
They know my walk
The perfect 45 degrees my hips sway
booty circling my waist like a protractor
I'm all that
Whistles and whispering
Praises curses
Worship and hate

Don't bother me none that they don't know my name
They know my talk
The smooth melody of my voice
The sweet humming of my vocal variety
The distinction of my verbiage
And choral bombast
Clarity and flash of white
With every conundrum alliteration and aphorism
I'm all that

Don't bother me none that they don't know my name
They know my mind
Quick and sharp
Million dollar ideas
Bounty of beautiful fantasies
Creativity and diversity
Divine ideology
Globally manicured
Cured for greatness
Attention to detail
Blossoming aneurism of charismatic dramatics
Polished politically correct in exact proportions of sensuality
Taken in doses overdoses
Dangerously anchored in righteous momentum

NUDE

Picking up speed and colliding into social scenes serene and
Ha. Don't bother me none/ not even a little bit
that they don't know my name

Suspension

Feeling the naughtily haughty frame of fortune
giving in to my inhabited habitual craving for the rising
Up and sturdy ready and willing
We are ready for the giving
In your eyes I find the solace of sanctity and
To that I yield myself
My fortress is broken and you enter my grace with the force you stare
The stare from your eyes
Your wise and open eyes
The rise the rise
The way you rise
The rise is all up in your eyes

NUDE

Starting New

Checking the time going crazy with my life's lines
Reeling in the bate sifting thru the hate
things still bug me
looking for someone to hold love kiss and hug me
I'm condemned to an everlasting memory to kill me softly
not a posh dwelling but a plush incant
wash off me

I deal with the losers

put u on a pedestal to be pleased
I get the backlash and then no relieve
I pour on ur feet jasmine and clover
I burn for ur sins and repent for u over and over
The commencement has come to graduate my pain
rinse away the hurt hatred putrid disdain
Frown lines embedded deep in yesterday's skin
The shallow part of my heart holds back the mend
Junky janky friends of whom u have no need
Back in my place a queen must take the lead
New to this journey amongst old friends
Time to erase her from life and begin to make amends
A scorch mark where her name used to be
Now to the future for us plus one the brand new we

NUDE

I been loving you

It's like I been knowing you forever
It's like we were together in another life
Spinning into every existence
Showing our love to the other
Tattooing my body on yours/ yours on mine/ your soul into mine
my soul into yours/ you on me

Inside me all over and around me
Digging me
Like
Like we are each other's air
Like I can't breathe without you

I remember those nights
Long dark nights
College dorms all the rooms mine and yours
I hear your heart laying on your heartbeat laying on your breath
Smelling you
Boy you make me laugh
Boy you make me cry
Boy you make me dream
Boy you make me live
I know dark rooms music and
I remember feeling your soul dancing and rubbing and touching
Feeling you like that
I remember my fantasies
You giving me the night and you exploring the inner me
I remember tears of joy
My first love
My long time thing
The father of my child

NUDE

Evolution's creation

I stand over myself and look at my sleep deprived rest stage looking for the inner moments that peer through the stain glass view of my heart throbbing in my transparent chest cavity so thrown back like Dos Equis on Easter celebrating the honesty of what I belong to, to what dream I belong I'm up on my crème banana brûlée fondly finding the sweetness in these bi-hearty times split between coming and coming twice forgetting how doubly manicured the seconds are around my sensuality decades of sounds yearning to be set free and fiends crave the melody escaping from my lungs diaphragms arrange the protection of sweet notes made to be released

Devoured by my satisfaction
Satiated devastated blown deviated and out of control
I've exploded into the moments of crinkled sweat stain sheets/ white walls holding the memory of my body's distortion proportioned to take everything it's given this is my evolutions creation I wasn't always this way timid not nearing exploration not even of my own not even of another of me no daring except with few unended attempts private moments public domains the only attempts young in age no real end no definitive peaks this has been my evolution's creation

NUDE

Southern goddess

I walked a dusty dirt road yesterday
My feet were dusty black and dirty
The dust swelled up around my ankles embedded itself between my toes and in the crevices of all ten toenails
I lifted my dress and let my thighs feel the heat of the summer and let the wind glide around my knees
my Afro blew in the wind and I watched the butterflies enjoying me
loving my chocolate skin glowing golden under the southern sun
I smelled the sweet honeysuckle fantasies giving life to my Sunday waking my senses
making me to believe I was alive
The pollen-filled flowers growing more jealous of me cuz the bees found me better than honey
and abandoned the flirty frenzy of pollination to buzz kisses as they passed me
curious and consistent
Favoring my pecan tan and buttery brilliance
I was kissed by the sun's southern side
Southside pride and African brand
a woman made of ten thousand women from the Yoruba tribe
the mother Yemaya
I've sucked from her breast
and my soul has grown becuz of Oyas sword of truth
I'm realized becuz the deities of story building springs truth into my reality
and I'm the woman strong
the woman proud
the woman resilient

NUDE

the woman powerful
the woman praised by her man
The woman adored by her child
the woman southern and salty from beautiful drops of sweat across
her strong forehead
for today's work has been done and tomorrow begs her presence
for it's labor
her legs bowed and strong carries her boldly to her home

NUDE

In the nude

Look me in the eye
Do you see the tears I cry?
Do you see truth or a lie?
Do you see a novice or mastermind?
Is the depth of my inner being what you're trying to find
Can you feel the struggle of my everyday grind?
Don't take spite don't rewrite or ignore the fight
My secrets aren't sublime
They aren't dormant in my mind
Take a journey through my time

Come, let me show you
Naked in your sight and I don't have to know you
In the nude unclothed right before you
Open your mind to who I am I won't ignore you
Ill awaken your senses and my seductive grace will adore you
I'll penetrate your thoughts make your existence fulfilling you'll be begging for more, you/ won't want to let go
Pressed forward yearning, for there's beauty in loves woe
There's room in my bosom for you to grow
Inside and out and here, it is so
Immediate impactful and contentious

I'm who I am not so pretentious/

Thus bemoaned you will come to know
    My life's silhouette...in the nude

NUDE

Contentious Repentance

Copious in a stark world of irrelevance
She shines of iridescence
marred and magnified

She is sultry and unjustified

She speaks:
I swear I wasn't gonna let him in
Give him room or drink his blend
I glorified in my revolt and am tortured in my loins

She hasn't been touched or rocked gently at play
She forgot the feeling the time and the day

She longs for simplistic pleasures and things of the sort
She yearns for manic moments convulsions to consort

She speaks:
I swear I would live past his memories his mind and scent
I will let them go only staring to see where they went
I strain my thoughts to spread eagerly over time
But wasted in this moment is my only peace of mind

Copious in a stark world of irrelevance
She shines of iridescence
marred and magnified
She is sultry and unjustified

NUDE

Feeling myself

Soooo....

Which building u lookin' down on me from, u bum?
Hope it ain't too high cz that'll be the one u gon' fall from

Like a bullet from a smokin' gun
I'm so hot we don't even need the sun

All my haters know the deal
Shame on you if u think u real
All that hatin' won't pay the bill
But listen I can tell u just what will
This grind right here I'm on
Ain't nobody gotta put me on
Future so bright I shine in the dark
Success so high pitch make ur dogs bark
I can't stop won't stop
'Til I get the champagne life, bottles to pop
And I don't even need a taste
I'm not even runnin and I'm winnin the race
I can do this in my sleep its second nature to me
I done turnt this thing into a full feature movie
You can't catch up, u too far behind
Just wait 'til the dust settles before tryn to mimc this grind
I'll be somewhere u won't find
Oh wait I'll b at the top of that building you fell from the first time
They keep sayin' my ego too big
But I'mma headliner I don't do the small gig
I keep tellin' 'em I'm in this to win
Just tryn to Stack my ends
I can't be mad if u don't wanna be my friend
Raw visions sittin' pretty with a big ass grin
Gotta Louis just to put my lip gloss in

NUDE

High profile it ain't a dream to me
I'm climbing to the top where I'm supposed to be
But I can see u hate that and want me to lose
That's gonna be hard for me cz I m paying my dues
Pardon me oh do excuse
While I step on you with my Jimmy Choo's
I've been going at this far too long
To let U kill my motivation. Wrong!
All that hatin' ain't good for u ya know
If u haven't noticed it tends to make u slow
If u come and I know you'll show
Fyi:. all the ushers already know
All haters must sit it in the back row
Don't block the supporters who care
Cz when the curtains open they recognize the greatness up there
I won't let y'all off that easy cz I know u see it too
This kinda shine ain't for everybody the chosen is few
Y'all just wish y'all can do it like I do
And I Wish I could stay and chat but hey I'm thru

Time's up for u haters no more cookies for u
Making u look dumb is always tons of fun
But I'll let u get back on ur job
This girl's got the world to run

NUDE

Hold us down (an ode to hip hop)

You rocked da beat
Took so many from the slums and stood 'em up on their feet

And gave 'em a kings speech

Valleys to vacate and mountains to reach
Whispered beats from da streets in their ear
Told them they had nothing to fear
Wiped the lonely tear drops from their forgotten faces
Gave them vengeance in lyrical places
Showed them the hustle is greatest on the pavement of paper
Made gun smoke disappear like water of the vapor

Turned vandal into art from heart
Created a place to run a place to end and a place to start
Pens and pencils lines that rhyme
Ballers without balls hustlers without time
You let them purge the secrets of the streets
Spit on vinyl written on the sheets
You put hope in awkward killer minds
You replaced guns and knives with grinds
You opened the hearts of eyes that were blind
Those who only saw red
found comfort in wordology and love for the dead

You replaced dope with hope
Gave Masters to beginners with hard enough lines
to crack the codes of the toughest street minds
You believed in them when they were alone
You gave them shelter when they had no home
Gave them food when they went without
Showed them the light when they wanted to doubt
Showed them what music was really all about
Gave them the get up and go

NUDE

Gave them the backbone when they slumped too low
You brought the melody to dull notes
When they were sinking, your creativity provided the floats
So here's to hip hop for always holding us down
Even with language barriers u gave us sign language like the peace sign and the pound
Thanks hip hop for holding us down
Unlike the 9-5 u gave us sanity cz u have no bounds
Give it up for hip hop for always holding us down
Unlike credit u have no limits so with u we can't drown
Hip hop ur always holding us free spirited creative beings down
At least in this nation we can all wear a crown
Big ups to hip hop for holding us down

NUDE

What things could be

You make me smile somewhere
Deep inside
You give me the morning
I slept anticipating through the night
I awoke to your morning glory
To open dreamless eyes
And behold the very thing
Missing from the night

I terminate thoughts of usurped pleasures as if it is a cardinal wrong to place my mind in a district where restrictions are restraints on our love

As if our love cannot reproduce abundance and adequate consumptions of love in its purest, rarest form

For you
I've dared to dance the moon from crescent to full

And brooms un-jumped
Cascades of fallen rain
Suites in island bliss for honeymooners and crooners
Await me in my awakened dreams
You are the perfect sunset and the melody of the waves crashing onto my desert island fulfills my life's destitute places and happiness is the conclusion to my beautiful story

NUDE

So Sick

I am so sick

So sick
Sick
Of this gender specific love
This love thing
This thing that ain't got rules
This love that makes me the ass the mule
the middle of the night fix satisfaction fuel
Let me challenge these fools to a duel
Where are the mandates?
Penalties consequences
Let's just think about it and come to a consensus
Men get off Scott free
They don't suffer the trauma of heartbreak and misery
At least not like the ladies
They don't bleed monthly and they certainly don't have babies

So when the next dude says its not you it's me
Baby
I'mma tell him to take his behind to hades

I'm afraid I'm an advocate of feminism
I just hate male dominism
And all the isms that idolize the gism

NUDE

Guessing

Hey sweet love
Guess what?
There's much to learn
To take in
To know
And be thus transformed
But in guessing know that here lays the secret to life

In the middle of a meadow
The trees bending in
The wind around my ears
Whispers of autumns sweet rosebud breath
The day weeps the seasons
Tears dew drops and stains

Hey you
Guess what?
In all the world there's much to gather
To consider
To believe
And in disbelief there's much to discover
But in guessing know that here lays the secret to life

To love you
To have you love me

The culmination of the airs we breathe that adds beauty to the wind that blows elsewhere and makes lovers out of unbelievers
    Strengthening the capacity for loving and building the bridge between hearts
So my darling as we spin in the air we create let me sing into the wind what my heart writes and my body bellows the music for us to dance to

NUDE

Step
By step
By step
In step
With the rhythm of our beating hearts
You have the melody
Melodic and mellow
Hello love
Can I have you?

All of you now?

NUDE

Last night

I don't write these words. I live and breathe onto the sheets

Tablets of disdain and pain passion from beneath the sheets
motions of motions that aren't so discreet
In brief
My testimony of deep deeps
Southern sadness dirty jokes
Mixed bastards and silly creeps

Jonesing for what I had last night
A delicacy fit for my appetite
I didn't stop but I put up a fight
I didn't want him to win
But not as bad as he wanted in
I didn't want to sin
But not as bad as he wanted to win
I followed my heart tried to run
But he wasn't finished he wasn't done
I followed my fantasy and gave him me
I found my point of no return for a fee
The cost of time
The cost of memories
I can't forget
The cost of I can never say I have nothing to regret
I saw a new world where a part of me lives
I saw something else that part of me gives
From a different place I never go
This locked away place my soulmate will never know
Unkept unholy undone unkept
After a night like last night I only recall how I wept
How each night after how little I slept
Last night was
One night that was
The last night

NUDE

Suspended in time

Suspended in time
Going in circles
Losing my mind
Stop
Rewind
Suspended in time
Stop going in circles
Can't get too far behind
Stuck in this haste
Trying to save face
But the damage is done
Begging reality to replace

My imaginations fail

NUDE

Wild flower

Hear this Prophetic prose
From the concrete grew this wild rose
I'm Short but long in thought
I finished your sentence the one that you fought
Long and hard to say
I may be gone for a minute but
Here's where I stay
Excuse me please but if I may
Use a crucible to loosen you cause these words is what I slay
No dungeon dragons forcing my mind to stray
I take hold of the words and mold em like clay
I'm like blue fire in the kiln no I don't play
Sharpen your skills like a number two pencil
cuz there's only one way
Don't fake raise the stakes be true and just pray
I don't come for you cz it'll be militia day
These words is hot so put 'em in an ice tray
I woke knowing today was gonna be a good day
Someone's mad cz the same bed they awakened in is the same one they will lay
I can be sure of myself now put that shit on replay
I'll join the league of greats that's with no delay
My mind is in g5 flight mode so my wheels don't fight the freeway
Instead I soar in my thinking and forfeit common relay
Running and gunning trying to beat out the rest and weigh
In like a heavy weight no falling in the gray
Area of unknown not being a common denominator perpetrating just to sway
The mind of a judge but I'm straight knowing Gods the only way
I sleep peaceful at night no napping in the day

NUDE

Keep my eyes focused so sharp
I can separate the butter from the Shea
See words run ramped in my head
and I won't stop my flows until God pronounces me dead

A disappointment

A devastated debate between the heart and mind
leaves me cold and beaten by the victory of the reality of the
present state of mind
my disappointment at the appointment where desperation and
negotiation meet my ever so slight attempt to fracture the hardness
that develops in the void of usual tendencies

born to create passion and pleasure

to bring about bliss in stagnation and flavor fondness with activity
of bodies intertwined to elicit provocativity meant to soothe the
unbearable bearing of complexities vexing me perplexing and
exing out the memorialized effort

to provoke a moment that never came...

NUDE

Sister to sister

You make me laugh
Retardedly
You make me cry
Insanely
Whatever moves to be made

I think of you
Constantly etched in my mind
Are thoughts of making your life better
Twins I say
Even the three

I'm a maniac if someone dares hurt you

The boys included

The object of my deepest love
I'd die a million horrible deaths if something ever happened to you
I was born to protect you and guide you
and at times you guide me
I'd never disrespect you
And work like all hell to not disappoint you
Do everything in my power to make you proud
It's simply amazing watching you grow
I have extreme difficulty letting you go
You're my babies
You're my very first loves
The pride of my world
Shining stars
Your beauty is uncanny
My very own blessing
Undeniably the best I've ever had
So /when /if/ however/ you need me

NUDE

I'll fly to your side
Glide to your aide
Fight to
Tear down any and all obstacles to show you my allegiance
No light diminishes your luminary presence in my life
The creme de la creme
The butter on my waffles
I cannot /and absolutely will not/ live without my sisters

Positive

No negative
Out of my comfort zone

3 pluses
My heart glides past all I've known

I breathe in the reality of not getting a negative
and begin my 10 month trial
Quickened by thoughts of me never walking down the aisle
With my legacy I'd gladly do again This Without denial

NUDE

Nights without You

You came and you went and I wish you never did

the magnitude of this disappointment bleaches the colors of my
autumn and tarnishes the brightness of my spring
leaving me to solemn senses and disabled fond finds and happiness
I've sought in you
neglect/ you did/ of what could have happened and transitioned my
thought to reflect the negativity of a situation gone awry
and left to interpretation of outside investigators
and observed by well-to-doers existing just to give an opinion
My dominion is blown
The travesty of a seed not sewn
A direction not gone
Infinity has an end
The custody of my sanity is up for adoption
And I have no option but to be consumed by this drought
And bouts of cravings unsatisfied
The night lights come alive
And dance on my misery

NUDE

Addict

I carry with me all you left behind
my lips stain with passion and persistence
the air between our embrace nonexistent
never present is the time I think not of you

ever present is your complexity perplexing my body
sending me into manic compulsion of pulses

no deficit in yearning what profits my imagination /of coral lips
wiped to natural /and replaced by blushing cheeks /flushed bloody red
matching sinful toes and fingers alike

fingers that tattoo your back saying I was here/ and the secret of us
is kept silent by the walls surrounding our pleasure

NUDE

Love lead the way

You let me believe it was ok to love you

And experience how loving you will make me leave my comfort zone

You told me it was alright to take the next step to delight in the pleasures that lie within
You held out your hand and wanted me to follow you wherever you were going
It was you who held me when I was scared and when I cried
It was you who promised to follow through
So I crawled out of my shell of resistance and was naked for you
I danced under the moonlight and showed you all of me

I held nothing back

I opened up for you/ and allowed you entrance into me/ into my world/ and let you navigate through the walls of my fortress

Amid my vitality you filled me and lay roots in my privacy
You became apart of me and left your spirit to dwell inside the vicinity of my divinity

NUDE

Too young to grow

I awoke this morning mad at me and scared and alone

I didn't do nothin' bad. I promise I didn't. Lil Roy wanted to kiss me but I told him no. I said, "no lil Roy kissing makes you have babies. You know that's what they say" but nah you know I ain't believe that no kinda way.

But what is goin' on? Am I dying? Did I get cut? No can't be. I ain't feel no pain so what can it be? I heard mama say it's a matter of time but it can't be for me. I aint but 10 and I don't even look at lil boys or even grown up men. They be lookin' at me but I ain't returning none of them whistles and stuff.

Can't fight 'em. Mama hate when I get rough. I ain't but ten goin' on eleven. My mama said them whistling men goin' to hell not heaven but what about me? Cuz I done started bleeding down there. Why me man? This ain't no kinda fair. I ain't get a chance to even grow boobs so I must be gettin' punished but what did I do?

I always give my dollar in church...well except last Sunday. Maybe that's why! God I hope you don't let me bleed 'til I die! I promise next Sunday I'll give my dollar and I promise not to lie.

People prolly gon' know cuz Suzanne started bleeding and she put on a show talkin' bout she a woman now and that she can make babies cuz now she know how but she be spyin' on her big sister and peakin' in on her when she with that mister. So I'm sure she know more'n me cuz I only seen a lil boys thing when we was all at the creek and he had to go pee. Outside of that I don't know much and I don't care to know nothin' bout sex and such.

NUDE

I like racin' boys and winning, not bein' up in their face skinning and grinning. That's for lil fast girls like Molly, who even think about Santa Clause in other ways than jolly; her and Lil Missy and Lil Miss Holly. I bet they bleed too cuz they a bit older; got me by a year or two. Man I don't wanna bleed and be a grown up girl cuz boys lie and try to promise you stuff they can't give like the world. They like you one minute and not the next. And Shyanne said if you don't wanna have sex, they get mad and say you they ex. They only like pretty girls; not girls like me with knobby knees and tight curls. And If your eyes ain't colorful they don't look at you. So I must be ugly cuz my eyes shol ain't blue. So I need to stop this bleeding cuz I don't wanna deal with none of that stuff. I wanna keep racin' boys and take my chance with mama, cuz I like being rough.

NUDE

Love reality

Heavy artillery bombs like on Hiroshima
devastating like race relations
this love thing is a big deal/ a big situation
basking in the sun of reality
the rays of it's brightness spreads in totality
and touches the inner outer and all
some make it through untouched/ most fall
it's humble demand makes a mockery of our so called humility
challenging our Humanity save the alternate possibility
when we are summoned to collect our two dollars and go
having not been burned and having nothing to show
fear of defeat got us shaking at the knees
fevers of 104 degrees
our mind trying to be our hearts referee
we are slaves to love/ from it nobody's free
Loves unholy decree
spoils from it's side effects
cold hard killers and withdrawn emo rejects
souls dying inside like jungle rot
trying to imagine the hell they're in as not being hot

NUDE

Jazz got the blues

I'm lost love life love

Take mercy on me
Blue grass moans
Gettin' deep inside me
Hip-hop homes
Focused on/ in/ into Ella
These be mo' betta blues
Got 'em flippin' on the mattress confessin' I'mma fool

Fake phony one night only groove

Encrypted screams and dim red shut blood shot eyes
Slow thick pours until their conscious dies
hard hit long puff' til their brain fries
hidden behind Dolce and Gabbana goin in for the win
my Gucci binge taking the bulk of my sin
Hustle hustle real hard
Don't let the competition in
Hustle in my sleep
Don't know how to make it end
maybe the answer's at the bottom of this bottle of gin

Damn she goin in

Black hands on my ebony skin
Low soft sound of lovers and friends
Typically Plays plays in the background
Ok we done can I have my love back now
I'm rude but then I love the fact how
I always seem to have your back
Love like crack

NUDE

Don't know how to act
All caught up thrown off track
Up in this joint blowin' stack after stack

Iniquitous cry

I breathe in iniquity
And swallow the sin

I pray God please don't let me feel so much pain
I hide my feeling in my groin
I am brought into this life with solemn grace
I am the woman I know to be
Dangerous with persuasion
I was promised a king
I crave to know the passion of pursuit and capture with my hands
the heart of a lover

Soulmate

I've met my soul and mated with him/ and I am his and he is mine
Forever indulging and forever has no time
No one else measures up to the abundance we share
There's not much chance at discovering a love so rare
But where true love resides
Trials come and tribulation hides
There is then a battle of hearts
To get to wed our futures and play our parts
And we'd fight without retreat for our hearts to win
We've been through and beyond and laid in sin
The thick of the chain holding us here
cannot be broken thus we love to not fear
For we are bound by our love
We've managed to believe/ going further above
fulfilling hopes dreams and fantasies alike
In the bliss of every moment with you I'd share every night
waking up to you at every morning's light

NUDE

Grace&Mercy personified

Staring at the beauty of grace and mercy personified

She breathes and her chest moves delightfully to the rhythm of the heavenly songs sung by angels in flight
Her breath dainty and new
Clean without blemish

Her skin smooth without flaw

What have I done to deserve such regal beauty and divine creation created in the image of perfection?

The possibility of description is none
and inevitability takes its place
She is what she is
An angelic perception of grace and mercy personified

NUDE

Love to be made

My tongue's tied I can't even speak
You kiss my lips and my knees get weak
My ears burn with lusty conjunctions
immobilizing my bodily functions
Serene sultry whispers of romance
and all's left is the mood to enhance
Tryna hold back but damn I just can't
I'm queen of the Nile as my river flows
Tryna check myself before I lose control
The air drenched with the scent
My arms bent at the wrist
Tryna get space between us before the night is spent
Before my frustrations I uncontrollably begin to physically vent
High and swollen I begin to feel heat from head to heel
The pulse and the need
The heat gathering sweat forms like a bead
between my breasts waiting for your lead
A hunger pain waiting for you to feed
Supple and erect
The passion's easy to detect
The moment becomes so easy to perfect
Let's make love the way we used to
Let's do the things we used to do

Let our passion flow and fill up the room
Making the walls sweat until the place is filled with our perfume

NUDE

Burnt out/wildfire

My senses go off
Like a fire alarm
To prepare me
Prepare me for more
Than what I think it might be
The smokes so thick
I can beat it with a brick
I inhale the smoke
And it's like I'm on dope
I can't even breathe
Like smokin' on trees
I become high
The heat index
Of my body's temperature rise/
My skin so damp
sweat gathers between my thighs/
Pressed together
tightly at the knee/
A thermometer can't count the height of this degree/
Like a wildfire u burn through my mind/
U bring the heat and send chills
Down my spine/
A fire like this cannot b controlled/
U come direct erect hard and bold/
I can't stop/ but I drop/
down and roll/
Parched in need of a drink

NUDE

Don't have to be cold/
This fire's got me bothered and hot/
It's got me acting like something I'm not/
Meeting the fire starter
And there's no time to waist/
He's the head of the game/
Strong and quick thick with perfect aim/
A good indicator of the weather
Like the main vain/
I show no fear
Cause I too have a good brain/
Ring the alarm the fire is insane...
As the sirens grow loader/
I feel the pulse from the inner to the outer/
As the sirens peak/
I feel the strength just before I get weak/
Just at the end of it's route/
Just before the fire goes out/
The water travels through the hose/
Exploding from the tip
The climax grows/
Taking my highs back down to lows/
Burnt out

NUDE

Flight pattern

Gravel beneath my feet
but I'm flying in the sky

I've brought the ground up with me
And I didn't have to try

love twin

She lays without effort

                         and falls into my soul /

 She is a part of me

God's work

He placed a hand at the nape of my neck and told me to take a deep breath

He hasn't told me to exhale yet

Suspended in a deep breath

My work is undone

NUDE

Tempted

Prepared for ignorant bliss

I give morale a forehead kiss

And be not gentle with my steps

I take a steady pace toward the deed of dirt I'm bound to do

And thus tread not lightly on slightly worn territory where whence I had been

and dare to return to what I've felt in sin

and sinfully delighted no warning blighted
and heeding not to trusted dignitaries
but placing safety and sanity in well worded obituaries
no tertiary thought to sweep me into my right mind
tonight I lay with the other side
and try with my might to remember my vow

Passion

I breathe heavily the fume

I sweat
I arch
I trace
I climax

I cry heavily the tears of gloom

NUDE

Unclaimed property

Antiquitous woman where's your glory
Why hangs your head so low
What's your story
Where's the dignity
Why don't you shine
Whoever has your heart has too your mind
Virtuous woman why hast thou no virtue
Where's your gifts -what things are owed you

Why don't you shine
Instead of walking the front
You fall behind
Whoever has your heart has too your shine

Government assistance

Hot rooms
White walls
And long lines
babies run ramped
throw fits
and whine

Baby mamas
No daddies
And Workers unkind
No breaks
No compassion
And you're treated like you've
no mind

NUDE

Done

It matters to me
What doesn't to you
It matters to me the things you do

I'm overwhelmed
Oh god why
I can't figure it out
So I cry

I lift my head for solemn peace to fall
You know this not but I'd rather erase it all

Second Chance

My heart abounds from the ashes of despair
Like the phoenix it rises
Waiting for someone to care
It holds to the hope not wasted on whom it despises

NUDE

Re-religion

Some never realize a better way and never take the time to pray
A god they seek
But this way they will always be weak
Their many from which to choose
Making their debts higher and higher becoming their dues
The rule is there's only one
And He is the begotten son
Taken to The pool of many
Causes lost souls or the righteous-less ones to go without any

Like
The relation of a Haitian nation

Not knowing where their faith went
With the undetermined determination of the eternity their souls to be spent
Some never realize a better way and never take the time to pray
But giving their prized lives and souls despise
Bears unholy hearts and dead cold eyes

There's no quick fix or way around what's required
Reach heavens gate and it'll say no quick fix angels for hire
They've all been fired

NUDE

With a smile

(a feminine approach) inspired by We Wear the Mask by Paul Laurence Dunbar

With a smile she leaves thoughtless pressures for the mind to think
All smiles wear she even on destructions brink
Her heart torn and bruised and battered
She'd rather smile than think of the latter
No idea what the end will hold
It seems a smile is all the more bold
Encrypted phrases spoken in her eyes
The bottom line is with a smile she covers what beneath it lies

The ending?

Angelic pressed persuasion dedicated to the way we deal
And I miss the feeling

I'm seeing clouds pass to open a path for the sun

increased breathing
harassing the diluted air
the reminiscence of your missed scent
polluting the environment that houses where I sweat
two sounds of decree mumbles
humbled moans
begging and yearning

wrapping us up and pressing our bodies

                                             how does this end?

NUDE

Freely freeing me

Just as I start to look/ to see/ to free what I call my me
Un-trap my mind and my destiny
There's the clandestine way the world has of letting us know
just how reality is just so   real
                        just surreal

        and just so
          we know   that's just the way it goes
                                    The way it goes
                                            it goes
     the way the way of going
     the way the truth has of it's knowing

It, truth, has a deal with time   but not mine
Cz I'm suspended in it   it rewinds

and I adjust and lay my course to my dreams

                              not brick and mortar wooden or
steel studs and beams
I have begun to free me [and insanely so]
because I've begun to take the leap
                            I'm high but then again I'm deep
Mid way in the trajectory of a quantum leap
be it of faith
be it of divine intervention
be it of destiny
be it of the knowing
the belief in growing
                the tactic of never slowing
but showing improve making the move
taking the goal I expand and demand

NUDE

a larger territory
on no small scale but a bigger testimony
my story
from dust to glory
watch- see -behold no fake no phony
this here's my testimony
but bold
taking initiative taking control
as the new becomes the old
as my story is told
as the warmth turns to cold
as the shy meager man becomes the bold

NUDE

True beauty virtue

A woman's true beauty virtue…

Dies when her mind yields no trace of believing in herself/ a woman must ripen her thoughts/ face the multitudes of grainy proportions to the sun and grow/ she should harvest her emotions according to the proper seasons/ her crop should produce the wisdom of years untold and picked by virtues own/ she should bear the fruits of the spirit and know this of her season…

Blooming in the fortitude of sensualities/ divinity diminished/ weeds of great resistance are uprooted by her el shabazz stride/ lion of Judah pride/ an heir to the Most High/ higher thoughts and motives met in the sky/ an angel in disguise/ Yeshuwa's beloved bride/ her clear conscious collides/ with reality/ and thus makes dreams so now and tangible evangelical/ a revelation relation related to her destiny/ destined for the greatness to which she belongs and longs to attain/ God built a fortress around her brain/ so the beauty of her mind might be preserved/ and the mission to this greatness will be served/ and her true beauty virtue deserved

NUDE

Assurance

As my debts loom

the clearing of my mind comes from knowing a love like what we share

Though lines be blurred/ others be crossed/ and we still know no boundaries

Our endless love portrays an earth unshaken/ embodies pure blue storm-less seas/ and foamy ocean piers beneath a boardwalk traveled by lovers hand in hand/

Looking into your eyes I see forever/ and forever stares my soul into a calm assurance

Preggers

Saltine Crackers and lemons
So much water I'd just as soon die

More Preggers

I just can't stop crying
The tears just don't cease
Looking at the scale
Just doesn't give me peace

NUDE

Nauseous

Anxiously awaiting your arrival
Abounding Thoughts of us and our survival
My thoughts shift focus back and forth
My mind dances around the subject of you
You move slightly to remind me
Of the blessing you are to my life
And the reservation about being a mother and not a wife
Comes in
As your life has yet to begin
Then you fill me with such undefined joy from within
A developing heir a new next of kin
And I move from reservations to patience and I hasten to the point of no return
No turning back and only months of much to learn
Your existence restores my faith and mediates my thought
Regulating the shifts in the very areas of my life where I've fought
Makes me forget the special attention that I've sought
and provokes me to rub my belly
In profound satisfaction that there is no end to our surviving but that its more of a thriving
Your little heartbeat is a retreat making me vacate to beautiful destinations in my future that will yield more delightful insightful moments paid in full because of you and I'm so grateful because of you

The nausea subsides

NUDE

Body thoughts

I sing a song of crimson lights

I dance the volume of a moonlit earth and bright blue strokes on a ready canvas
ready for arousal
I'm loving you
I'm breathing your air
I'm feeling your touch left on my skin
In need of your strength
Your body and physique
I close my eyes and smell the scent of you
the scent of our silhouette and sweat
with every curl of my toes I arch my back and am met
with the glory of your lips
the passion of your kiss
Our bodies dance into rhythm and the beauty of our love
reaches heaven

Bound by perception I gain composure and desert my compromise and go back to supervising my life inside reality outside of my fantasy and wait for the moment they- reality and fantasy- collide into one another and your touch doesn't dissipate with the opening of my eyes

NUDE

Sleepless nights

Caught up in the moment of undesignated feelings

How do I express what I need when I feel the need to need what I want

So deep in this thing I cant breathe
Wanting desperately to resign from this funk

To create leverage for my happiness

I long and yearn and in return…a dead end emotion
With what sentiment do I receive what I've gone too long without?
The touch…your touch
An embrace…your embrace

Laced with the fittings that cling tightly to every inch of me…every breath
An uphill battle for intimacy
A course of struggles to burn my night with endless romance

To set free what has been locked away
and time releases endorphins of passion-filled fantasies
and braves each temptation
and flirts with each attempt to instill it's might in mystic morphine doses
of intoxicated toxic relations
 I've come to believe it will bring only more sleepless nights

NUDE

AWAY

Away

I've come to realize the meaning of the word as it makes manifest in my today/ in my now/ as now turns into forever/ and forever is indicative of the way things are.
We have seen waves/ and many reach our shores/ and wash away our beginning/ taking our castles out to sea/ buried in salt and water/ and cascades of decadent blue/ like long lost forgotten treasures/ be that they may but lost at sea is a tyranny of travels/ done/ and many moons/ over/ as the waves roll away beneath a pitch black canvas/ so does the pitch black moments that lay dormant in time/ throwing curses at what lies within/ as daylight penetrates the deep black/ and brings streaks of blues/ soft sherbets/ with warm tendencies to break up the solemn silence and loveless cold darkness

NUDE

Take lead

Flying planes pour down no positivity /like it rains pesticide for pest prevention/

paying special attention/ to intention/ dot dot dot/ to be rid and rebid an extension of demolition/ of which a wrecking crew lacks the vision of pursuit of the bottom line/ but keeps someone else's goal in mind/

Minds on mute/

No order to refute/

but follow through with the commands/ tearing down hearts and homes/ NOT built by man's hands/ but comes at it's greatest demand/ heroes to those who just don't understand/ but scared to be reprimand-ed/ and this being end-ed/ is their individual crusade for peace/ And war remains in hearts with ease/ and spreads like a disease/ because no one will stand up/ face the trials and tribulations of leadership/ take part in ownership/ of tomorrow/ but would rather be lost/ in today's sorrow

NUDE

Far away from home

A misdirected derelict of no mind
        time tested devotion sprung through my being
Penetrating where my blood runs warm

        Night turns to day and blue jays sing my secrets

Wayward of dewy daffodils that make markers for the way I've come

        Tree limbs hang loosely like liquid falls trying to hold on to me

Touching my shoulders and remembering my body

        a willow weeps in front of me unashamed of her sorrow
and beckons my open heart to speak
        and so I speak of my love
                my woes
and weep within to conquer the moments without
        and outside of where whispers win

        and moans begin
       and making love is the twin to my sin
Far away from home/ back out in the world again

NUDE

Conscious living

Blessed with the best

I am adorned with the headdress

Of conscious living
Blind to no future erection of unholy your majesties

ready to take the throne of forbidden places
no traces of wear and tear
of new devotions ready to be over/ ruled/ and under/ announced/

drawing in provocative dangers/ starved for awakening/ bound to their end/ and beginnings/ to start me where I should end/ and end me at my beginning/

leave me feigning for the midpoint of my journey/ where I was with accompaniment/

but shadows me with the truth of now/ and I was without you at the beginning/ and thus take refuge in the similarity of the end/ going out like I began

NUDE

Black Ice

Black ice ain't no friend of mine
                               I can't take what I need to get
where I need to go

 cz it's got it's way
                        it stands between me and where I must go
I ain't shy but it got me quiet as kept
                                 and no mind to try getting bold
guess I'll stay in my place and wait 'til it starts to cry
                                  instead of being just so cold

GN & GM

My dreams create rapid fantasies staying solid in my mind like a million galloping horses running me through /leaving imprints of what was once now/ but is now then and therefore passed /and past is present in the present/ wanting crescent moons to become new moons... I just want to say goodnight and then say good morning

NUDE

Answer to My Rebellion

Fear me
Fear she
The she within me
The magnitude of this moment

Makes me indulge in myself

For in my womb
Lies the answer to my rebellion
Resurrecting my restricted thoughts
And fulfilling my empty spirit
Thoughts so loud anything else I can't hear it

You're so close to my heart my brand new start you're the one
stable thing when my world falls apart
I am taken by the movement of your eager unknowing
And everybody knows just why I'm glowing

The miracle of you just keeps on growing
and I can hardly wait now that I'm showing

For in my womb
Lies the answer to my rebellion
Stretching my imagination
Enticing the way to my destination
My participation is the preparation to reach elation infatuation
perpetuated saturated in the reincarnate of a love thang

Swing low sweetest chariots blazing fires across the skies
For in my womb lies my truth no lies
but I know I am weak/ He is wise
I'm seeing truth through your new eyes
And it comes to no surprise

NUDE

that amongst living things some thing dies
inside to emerge from the ashes and rise
New pure true cure life without fewer interruptions corruptions
and spiked punchbowls placed where strongholds
and love folds to meaningless desire
You are my moth/ I am your fire
My unborn soulmate/ my one true future desire
I've reached a higher status of mind
Now in front no longer behind
You're the best find
Now I must leave my wretched self behind and grind

NUDE

Remembering you

You think we in love huh?
You really think love got us here ?
This be the moment of a lifetime of fear
To think we were only having fun
It's not fun Not knowing if you're the one
You know, the one

One like no other the earth the moon the sun
felt all special when you used to hug hold and kiss me
just knew you hated when I left and that you really missed me

You would look me in the eye and say baby I love you
Couldn't nobody tell me that it wasn't true
Waking up without you was a devastating nightmare
 If it didn't involve you I couldn't give a care
You were what I wanted you were what I needed
All the red flags the warnings I should've heeded
They're faded in the past but are ever so present
But you were my light and so luminescent
Possibly… the best I ever had… so effervescent
You could never be the past you were always my present
A conglomerate of love now I know to be lust
And all I gave travels to an end like us…back to the dust
Thus then and thus how
If I'd have known then what I do now.
I'll always remember you with what you left behind
Something always documented and never leaves my mind
You left me blemished not just with the time
Another mountain in my life for me to have to climb
Another problem that's so not sublime

NUDE

Another day another body falls victim to the crime
Another left to suffer the grit and the grime
Of another nigga feelin himself cz he's in his prime

First day of school

Nervous
Bobby socks and beads
The ones with the rubber bands
Boys and girls already holdin hands
Sho wish they have something good for lunch

NUDE

That's Life

I'll give my last
The last and the final

no morning to come that a breath would come forth to utter my name

beyond the brevity of sanctity and sanity

the very profanity of minds to think the thoughts of a world unknown
but to speak words of rebellion
the very rebellion that I've become
For surely I belong to another life
another body that inhibits another space
I'm attracted to nothing you've shown me

and on that note I've changed
not only my mind but my body
bc it moves so different
I'm so different

my mind thinks different thoughts

not like before
not like it was with you

have you any idea the ideas that ideally I idealize
for we were once/ and now I am no longer apart of the pair
I do declare
that I am hurt and abused by the 'that's life' mentality
the reality of where we are
and there's splendid time/ right here and right now/ to face our past
for each element to exist in every moment/ in beauty/ and in ugly
to memorialize what we've been

NUDE

I can't for the life of me until now remember a time I didn't die a million tiny deaths
to position my mind/ to position my heart/ away from you
for of you I have lived and breathed
to inhale/ and never to exhale/
to never let go of what in my dreams have been my possible reality

see my womanhood exists where my heart does
and they must both grow
my heart has been sent out like a hound to track you down
but such a dummy mission leaves behind a trail of unanswered questions
but then I somehow delight in the uncertainty/ the complications of love

Finding perfect

I lost perfection of my imperfection being perfect for you
these seasons are strange and new
so new like the morning dew
and what I've come to know as true
is the beauty of me being me and you being you

NUDE

Ladylike

For the edification of our souls
We will dare to do what we're told
Close our legs
And pull up our panty hose

And be ladies
Hear our speeches
Uplift our prose
Words bring wisdom
To what 'Asses' knows
There's really a method to our madness

And without us there's sheer sadness
We're not to be compared or dared

But heed this warning do beware
Our bowed legs arched backs
all things at which you stare and glare
is all in the message which we will share

walkin' holy

Blinded by the light which tells my name but not my story

U see, even God's own took flight and fell from glory
Every man demonstrates his cardinal sin

But not every man lives to see a beautiful end
Sometimes you will walk a green mile just to figure things out
A constant show-n-tell that's not what life is all about

NUDE

Green grass grows on both sides of the fence
And where ever wrong is you can always smell the stench

No matter the distance from the point of resistance but Christians are always on missions
Blessings and curses don't live in the same place but when they take off they seem to reach the same pace
Faster and faster ripping through time

Things to repent are never so sublime

Mixed breed

Black backs and blue baby blue eyes

Not too young and not too wise
Little tortured kittens mixed babies binkies and woven mittens
Saturday morning cartoons and cracker jacks
Blue baby blue eyes and black backs
Wish all they had to worry about
was being quiet during nap and trying not to pout
What products to use on that baby's two-type hair
We with all the worry
THEM without a care
A chocolate vanilla swirl
And it takes nine to pop out a caramel baby girl
With blue baby blues
And straightened curly cues

NUDE

I. Love. You.

I can take a million words and toss them in the air
And what comes back down ain't always fair
And what comes down it may be what my soul needs to bear
Trivial in my pursuit for just the right pair
Sometimes I speak them without a care
And sometimes I speak when there's nothing there
No matter the couple or triple to speak I dare
To say three words to you, my heart needs to share

Winter happenings

Slushy concrete/ red nose/ and damp bangs from expired ice fleeing sickled branches/ Little bundled babies barely showing eyes/ lost cats crooning waiting for a fireplace and warm lullabies/ birds no longer chirp from ahigh/ 'gone for the season' replaces their perch/ a storefront sign measured by the nonexistence/ and gone south resistance/ til the skies warm up/ from inside smoke fights it's way to an utter demise of sharing with the outside world/ the frozen skies take its expired heat

Country winter

Bring me that salt,
before I fall and break my good hip
unexpectedly slide and impermissibly flip
Without my good hip,
I can't bust a move and hit my world famous dip
So bring me that salt,
Cause all I's got left is my one good hip

NUDE

Mind made up

I reached the moment when loving u is the call I want to make/ I want everything to yield beautiful fruits and the labor is but a daunting task, done and over with, beyond existence and full of a non-future respect

Reproduction

This was made for me
It's my time
Watch out world cause here I come
I'm running steady running steady coming
Coming into this new me
A new me in this old world
A new me in a place

A place where I can be free

I dug deep into this heart of mine
I've inherited this new mind
I'm a surrogate mother to a renewed sense of self-indoctrination
to conceive what love has placed into me
A look through my eyes unveils a vulnerability/sensuality set a part
Sexuality set to start
I was born to love
I've been chosen to love

NUDE

Romanced

Love burrows deep in this place and dwells within these walls
Love brings me to a high
fills my nose with a sweet aroma as it falls
Ever so gently upon my breasts and rests
I have been romanced
Deflowered enhanced
I have been romanced
No longer a virgin
Romanced

Completely Incomplete

Completely old
Completely gone
Completely frayed
Completely slain
Go on to where u came from
Fragmented and saucy
Sanctifying my forbidden soul
Mercy and mayhem
The madness of this lust
I'm a creature like no other
I was brought forth from the dust
Here I stand in the perimeter of my own flesh
With my insecurities and feeling unblessed
Completely incomplete

NUDE

DeVIRGINated

Straight
Running
Deep
Intertwined
Into me
Deeper inside
Conquering feats
Running
Hard
Striking force
Loving between time
Layers of light passing through my thighs
Higher than the skies
Fake phony in disguise
Flying and fulfilling
Sweet remnants of willing
Short shots of Saffron spilling
Showering my flower
Amidst ruins of an ancient roman tower
Bereft of fortune a lonely dower
Sucking at the very power
Of the inside in between
Showering my flower
Divulged at the very instant
A token of forgiveness at mid stint
You miss it you kiss it
The affection you pissed it
Don't be so distant
This here is instant
Stop
Running
Stop crying
Laying facing down
Take it laying face down

NUDE

Finding u

I was so sure

Sure to find find a piece a piece of mind
I perfected being alone
My heart was looking for a home

Home grown and lonely

Wanting a one and only
I was scared of disappointment

Not knowing what us/ together/ and we meant
an appointment of a crushed grape anointment
I am in the moment I'm living it now
I remember when where and I remember how
I am finding time
I am finding truth
I am finding hope
I am finding these things
Becuz I found u

About us

When I hurt when I cry
You'll know I'll tell you why
I've got issues and the world ain't got my back
The very dominion of a heartless world surpasses my integrated mind
where two opinions reside and divide my emotions
I'm your woman and I believe in 'us'

NUDE

but when the faction of our 'us' is lacking
and we can't be called thus
and we're individuals and individually ascertaining individuality
your life, my life,
I ain't feeling that
so when the faction of our 'us' is on hold
please leave a message at the beep
and tell me what's wrong
beep
after loving so strong
beep
after it being so long
beep
this message shouldn't last that long
beep…

don't form your mouth to say some |other than truth| kind of words
prearranged in a fault full of thoughtful angst
so when the faction of our 'us' is on hold

I ain't feelin' that

Winter night

We grab hold of what we can and rush the door in a relay race with the biting wind quick on our heels
Hot cocoa loves on a deep mug and lips yearn for it's familiar warmth
The jealous wind wraps at the door forgotten and left behind
but we dine on liquefied chocolate desperate for the inside of a body escaping the winter
The winter is outside
and summer develops on the inside where cocoa dwells

NUDE

Overdose

I been shot up too many times
My veins is like the dope drive thru lines
Hat kindly cocked to the side
Hey sweet mama can I get a ride
I been dealing this shit too long
I knew from the start this shit was wrong
I am inky black
Steady tryna find what I lack
Don't know what I lost in this overdose
Done too many shots of love where am I supposed
To go to find what I lost
All up and down this way that way and what'll be the cost
This love thang got me twisted up and tangled
sweet and sour senses dangled right in front of my face
Someone slap me in the face
Wake me up to find the place
Where love faked me out
Took me out, wined, dined and them left me out
In the cold
Cold/ a place I know/ a place I hid
Somewhere that ain't even on the grid
where I can't find myself
To the cries of sanity I turn an ear that's deaf
It rains bullets in my neighborhood
and round here ain't nothin' good
I'm a fool to myself

Winter Night 2

Dirty white snow
Lumped by the road
Animals in hiding nowhere in sight

NUDE

Fragmented trees stuck without say
Hills created that never were
Icy patches blanket the way before travelers
sleepy from third shifts
Dirty wretched drunks
accompanied by ladies of the night in bare midriffs
Truckers with a long way yet to go
The cold night beckons a travesty for these
The branches tremble at the thought

Cold outside

It's cold outside
I want chocolate, hot
It's cold outside
I want what the wind ain't got
It's cold outside
Inside's my best bet
It's cold outside
I didn't pay the electric bill yet
It's cold outside
And sadly I'm just as he
Just as he who ain't got an inside to be

Old sins

I thought I could sleep off the stench of last night's sin
The trauma of waking to what I did

Stains my body and waits to make me relive the moment of insanity

NUDE

When I got weak and fell for the same old routine
He looked at my ass and yelled for my attention
He barked about my attitude and pulled up next to me
Showed me his flexors and jailbird tattoos
Wanting to impress me and get me again
But I had outgrown him and wasn't in love with the type
that couldn't be straight on an employment application
street pharmacist
my first and first to be thought of as love
the necessary childhood mistake
to make me grow up
I was in a weakened place
Love was unkind to me
Un betrothed
Empty gaps in my thinking
I was a sitting duck
Penetrable by slum ignorance
Back-wood grammar

The first was back for seconds

In his motor vehicle
Not driving of course
DUI, Suspension, Infractions, penitentiary
All synonymous with this street pharmacist
My first

Smooth talk and swagger

Saying sweet nothings
Promises, allocations with money earned on a pharmacist's budget
Familiar and desirable
Only in the moment
Only in lieu of previous fornicated failures
Unwed and broken
Just needed a fix

NUDE

I made excuses and met his hand in the air
Went his way and laid my burdens down
Put my weight on his shoulders
Evolved through my stages of pain and let him have the leftovers
The baggage
I departed from the love depot and gave him my bags
I checked out of his hotel after my unholy release of emotions
I left there and left behind my troubles

And took with me his
Crooked system

Systemic waste

    A world where race doesn't have a face
    Million dollar porcelain veneers sucking the bones dry

Economical distaste

Bland and flavorless in the mouth of the poor making haste
To get poorer and the rich get rich
The poor don't get rich quick/ But quick to get rich/ A quick hit to the wrist
A political risk
    It is to keep it real
Dollar $igns in the eyes/ promised prize
to disguise the truth and lie/
for honesty to lay down his life and die
patriotism is the key to sur-vive
ole red blue and wyyte
flying through the night
    giving proof that its still there
    but its soaked in blood/ rude/ crude/ and unfair
    what's the worth of a flag if the americans can't share

NUDE

the same privileged history

the sense here just don't exist to me
And see Columbus is just a thief to me
How you claim land that aint free
So what kind of god you supposed to be
To strap a detonator on your integrity
    And blow it up with your ego
    How far back can we go
Where justice and peace was ever the goal
MLK made strides but then he dies and the meaning gets old
    Panthers are black/ that's a matter of fact
And fists in the air
    Matches well with big ole kinky hair
and the stale scent of Mississippi burning flesh lingering in the air
    matches well with nature cause boy I swear
those who love trees
tell me the meaning please
    of 400 years worth/ of shame and discourse/
    predetermined explanations with no resource
to site/ although its there in black and white

Now Napoleon… is great but he ain't the right height
And the founding fathers could go fly a kite

    I don't have sympathy
    For a nation that can't bow out gracefully

I'd rather salute the black backs
    on which our nation was really built
The frail crinkly and broken hands that really helped sew the quilt
    Of stability and pride
    When I think of this kind of greatness I let the racism ride

NUDE

'Cause this is the source of real pride
    The source of real tears cried
    The source of entire races trying to survive
    I mean, how hard can it be to have motive and drive?
How hard can it be to let racism ride?
    Probably as hard as it was to see MLK and Malcolm X die
    As hard as Mamie Till cried
    As hard as Mahatma Gandhi tried

  Sometimes it's just too damn hard to let racism ride

Road to Stardom

  I fell asleep and I dreamed I was a queen
  I dreamed the lands were mine to rule
  And all bowed at my feet
  They worshipped the ground on which I walked
  They listened intently when I talked
  They hung on my every word
  I dreamed the stage was mine
  The lights shined
  On me and they watched me
  They loved me
  Every seat was filled every ticket bought
  Every paper magazine and station celebrated me
  I graced the world with my benevolent presence
  I gave face and batted my eyes

NUDE

I twisted my hips and their praise clung to my silhouette
It's my debut
I'm the star of my very own world
I love and they love me
I live for this moment
The curtains close
The director says that's a wrap
Its thrown to the editing floor
Cuts made rewrites and pickups help to mold the perfect picture
They're rolling
They yelled ENCORE
I'm on
Moving up the ladder becoming iconic
Every day and night begins to blend
Fame
Finally
Freedom
Every day and night begins to blend
Do I really want this?

NUDE

Transformed...a poem about motherhood

This motherhood thing...
Me a mother
A primary caretaker
Guardian of a life
With the strength of my ancestors
I take her in my arms and our hearts beat in tandem
Welcome to this world
She welcomes me into hers
I lift her up and dedicate her life to the creator
Blessed and honored
Adoration of her beauty
She suckles at my breast
Swaddled and meek
Fragile and dependent
This is my right of passion
My destiny unfolds
She relies on me for all her little new life requires
24 hours 7 days a week 365 days a year
My job is never done
My life will never be the same
I've given life to a beautiful little girl
She looks at me with fresh untainted eyes
And depends on me to teach her/ to show her/ to love her
But she teaches me/ she shows me/ she loves me

NUDE

I watch her everyday and am transformed
No greater love than that of a mother unto her child
But the creator's for the created
I know this love now
Motherhood…it aint for everybody
But it is for me

www.ingramcontent.com/pod-product-compliance
Lightning Source LLC
Chambersburg PA
CBHW071155090426
42736CB00012B/2339